D1479211

Eat To Live

*A compilation of information on food
from the records of Edgar Cayce's
clairvoyant readings.*

❧

PUBLISHED BY
THE EDGAR CAYCE PUBLISHING
COMPANY, INC.,
Virginia Beach, Va.

INTRODUCTION

The material contained in this booklet was taken from more than fifty individual clairvoyant readings given by Edgar Cayce. In all of these readings questions of a general nature were asked about diet. All of the quotations used here appeared at least three times and most of them were repeated dozens of times.

Everything that you should eat or not eat, according to the information in Edgar Cayce's readings, is not listed here. However, if you will study the data carefully, you will observe simple fundamentals of eating which may help you build a better body.

Throughout all information on health, as given in the readings, the keynote is *balance*. Nowhere is it stressed more than in suggestions regarding food.

The body is recognized as a vehicle for, and at the same time a projection of, the soul. The body's health plays an important part in the spiritual growth of the entity. It must not be pampered; its existence must not be denied; as a means of expression it should be an integral part of the WHOLE spiritual growth.

In adapting these suggestions for your own use be sure that you recognize them as outlines and general statements, indicative of principles. Your particular needs must be the basis for all decisions. Consider your type of activity, your environment and the degree of mental control which you have attained.

If this is your first introduction to the clairvoyant work of Edgar Cayce, we recommend some of the publications listed in the back of this pamphlet. We call your special attention to THERE IS A RIVER, The Story of Edgar Cayce, by Thomas Sugrue.

When Edgar Cayce died in January 1945, he left over 30,000 clairvoyant records and reports from individuals and physicians. Based upon the benefits derived by thousands of individuals from these readings, the work of studying and publishing abstracts and cross-section reports is going forward under the Association for Research and Enlightenment, Incorporated, of Virginia Beach, Virginia. The information is characterized by its simplicity, well-roundedness, saneness and, most important, by the results of its use.

The majority of the selections included in this pamphlet were taken from a collection prepared by Mae Gimbert and Harmon Bro, former Staff members. Working without an index they performed a valuable service in checking these oft repeated, generally applicable health suggestions.

—HUGH LYNN CAYCE

ASSIMILATION AND ELIMINATION

*"There should be a warning to all
bodies as to such conditions; for if
assimilations and eliminations were kept
nearer normal in the human family, the
days of life might be extended to whatever period as desired.. For the system
is built by the assimilations of that which
it takes within; and it is able to bring
resuscitation so long as the eliminations
do not hinder."*   No. 311

*"The best laxative is a balanced diet
...."*   No. 457

SUGGESTIONS FOR BALANCED MEALS

These outlines were combined from the following cases:

Nos. 1523 — 3224—3823—257—935—1568—2602—1131—574—311.

BREAKFAST

Whole grain Cereals, with Milk and Honey*

or

Citrus Fruit Juice (Orange with a little lime, or grapefruit with lemon) **

or

Dry Cereals, with Berries or Fruit

or

Raisins, Dates, Figs chopped together * * *

or

Figs and Dates cooked with a little corn meal

or

* Honey was frequently recommended instead of sugar.

** See section on AVOID THESE COMBINATIONS

*** This was given many times as a very excellent food combination:

[7]

Yolk of egg with crisp bacon if desired
Toast (brown or whole wheat bread), or
Rice or Buckwheat Cakes
Cereal drink, or Coffee without milk or
cream

LUNCH

Vegetable Broth

or

Vegetable juices (Use juicer and combine
to taste)
Raw Vegetable Salad
Suggestions: Tomatoes, lettuce, watercress, radishes, spinach,
carrots, cabbage, etc.
(Grate or shred, combine
to taste).
Dressing: Olive oil or
vegetable oils, no vinegar
or
Fruit Salad (Combine as desired—without
raw apples)
Seafoods
Brown, whole wheat or corn bread
Cereal drink, Coffee or Tea without Milk
or Cream.
1 cup Black or Assyrian Figs, chopped, cut
or ground very fine
1 cup of Dates, chopped very fine.
½ cup of Yellow Corn Meal (Not too finely
ground).

[8]

Cook this combination in 2 or 3 cups of
water until the consistency of mush.

Such a dish as a part of the diet often will
be an aid to better eliminations, as
well as carrying those properties that
will aid in building better conditions
throughout the alimentary canal.

Lamb, Fish or Fowl

or

Beef (occasionally)

or

Calf liver, brains, tripe or pigs' knuckles
(not pickled)—once or twice each week.

Vegetables—All kinds—Use three above
ground to one below; one leafy
vegetable to each pod variety.
Cook in their own juice.

Gelatin Salads with vegetables

Dessert—Fruit, raw or cooked (Cooked, not
raw apples are recommended).

or

Gelatin with all types of fruit.

or

Ice Cream—Test quality.

Bread and drink as above.

[9]

GENERAL SUGGESTIONS

The following suggestion appeared in different phraseology in a number of readings: ". . . It is well that the body not become as one that couldn't do this or that, or the other, or become as a slave to an idea of a set diet. . . ."

The readings advocated a balance of 80% alkaline producing foods to 20% acid types.

Plenty of water in relation to good digestion was stressed. Six to eight glasses full each day were recommended. Half a glass of warm water before breakfast each day, with an occasional pinch of salt, was also suggested.

WHISKEY AND TOBACCO

Q.—"Have personal vices such as tobacco and whiskey any influence on one's health or longevity?"

A." . . . . You are suffering from the use of some of these in the present, but it is over-indulgence.. In moderation these stimulants are not too bad, but man so seldom will be moderate. Or, as most say, those who even indulge will make pigs of themselves.. This over indulgence, of course, makes for conditions which are to be met. For what one sows, that must one reap. This is unchangeable law." No. 7033

FOOD VALUES

ALMOND

"The almond carries more phosphorus and iron in a combination easily assimilated than any other nut."   No. 1131

"And if an almond is taken each day, and kept up, you'll never have accumulations of tumors or such conditions through the body. An almond a day is much more in accord with keeping the doctor away, especially certain types of doctors, than apples."   No. 3180

APPLES

"To cleanse all toxic forces from the body eat nothing but raw apples of the Jonathan variety for three days, and follow with half a cup of olive oil."   No. 820

ARTICHOKE, JERUSALEM

The Jerusalem articoke, if not on the market, may be ordered for a few cents a pound from: The John A Salzer Seed Co., LaCrosse, Wisconsin. Keep the artichoke in a flower pot, or imbedded in the ground, so as to preserve them; they will not keep on ice, but need to be in the ground. Eat one about the size of an egg twice a week, once raw and once cooked. Cook in Patapar Paper so as to preserve the juice, and

[11]

mix the juice with the bulk of the articoke when it is eaten....after seasoning it to taste. Eat it with the regular meal, not by itself.... that is, do not make a meal off just the articoke ....by eating it between meals, or the like.

This type of articoke frequently recommended for diabetics carries sufficient insulin to be easily assimilated in this manner and is not habit forming.

BULGARIAN BUTTERMILK

"Bulgarian buttermilk, or fresh milk that is warm with animal heat is better than ordinary milk. They carry more phosphorous and more of those properties that are less constipating or are capable of acting more with the lacteals and the ducts of the liver, the kidneys, and the bowels themselves."   No. 560

CALCIOS

"*Calcios* is the best way in which to take calcium. It is more easily assimilated, and will act better with pregnancy than any type of calcium products as yet presented. About three times each week, at noon meal, eat a whole wheat cracker spread thinly with the Calcios."
No. 951

Calcios is distributed by: Colloidal Health Products Corp., Att. A. A. Nichoson, Greenvale, L. I., N. Y.

"At least once or twice each week sea foods may be taken, especially clams, oysters, shrimp or lobster....The oyster or clam should be taken raw as much as possible, while having the others prepared through roasting or boiling with butter...." No. 275

"Plenty of fowl, but prepared in such a way that more of the bone structure itself is used as a part of the diet in its reaction through the system; so that better reaction for the assimilation of calcium through the system is obtained ....Chew chicken necks, then, chew the bones of the thigh.

"Also have the marrow of beef. Eat such foods as vegetable soups that are rich in beef carrying the marrow of the bone, and....eat the marrow." No. 1523

"Keep plenty of those foods that supply calcium to the body. These we would find especially in raw carrots, cooked turnips, turnip greens, all characters of salads, especially as salads of watercress, mustard, and the like. No. 1968

"....the phosphorous forming foods are principally carrots, lettuce (rather the leaf lettuce....than the head lettuce) shell fish, salisfy, the peelings of Irish potatoes (if not too large)...." No. 560

[13]

GRAPE JUICE

Welch's grape juice was frequently recommended to aid in reducing weight. Two ounces of grape juice to one ounce of plain water four times each day (one half hour before meals and time of retiring) was the formula most frequently given. Nos. 2455; 2040; 619; 457; 2067.

POTATOES, IRISH

"For stimulating the growth of hair; First, do not eat Irish potatoes; this is, the pulp, but do eat the skins of same, and that which is very close to the skins. Also, the skins of apples (that are cooked, not raw), the skins of apricots and a portion of same, these supply elements for the activity with the thyroid, that produce for the body the activities of the hair, the nails, and those portions of the system. Use as a massage the crude oil, cleansing same with a twenty percent solution of grain alcohol; not denatured or wood alcohol, but grain alcohol; and massage into the scalp small quantities of white vaseline. These will stimulate growth.   No. 826

VEGETABLES

"Do not have large quantities of any fruits or vegetables, meats, that are not grown in the area where the body is at the time it partakes of such foods. This will be found to be a good rule to be followed by all...."   No. 3542

LETTUCE

"Plenty of lettuce should always be eaten by almost everybody, for this supplies an effluvium in the blood stream that is a destructive force to most of those influences that attack the blood stream. It's a purifier." No. 404

TOMATOES

"More of the vitamins are obtained from tomatoes than in any other one growing vegetable." No. 180

YELLOW VEGETABLES

"Be sure that each day there is sufficient B-1 for the adding of the vital energies. Those vitamins are not stored in the body as A, D, and G but it is necessary rather to add these daily. All those fruits and vegetables that are yellow in color should be taken: oranges, lemons, grapefruit, yellow squash, yellow corn, yellow peaches and beets." No. 2529

WINE

"Wine taken in excess, of course, is harmful; wine taken with brown, black, rye or whole wheat bread alone is body, blood, nerve and brain building." No. 821

[15]

WORKING HOURS

Q.—"How can I develop the ability to work long hours, and what are the best hours for work?"

A.—"When the fewest number of people are thinking about work is the best time to work, for any individual. Hence, to answer the other question, by raising resistance to illness in the body, the body will be able to control the hours of labor physically and the hours of labor mentally. Remember that. . . .all work and no play will make just as dull boy as all play and no work, and will make one eventually worthless to self and to that which one . . . . would desire to accomplish.

"Best that every individual. . . . budget his time. Set so much time for study, so much time for relaxation, so much time for labor mentally, so much time for activity of the physical body, so much time for reading, so much time for social activities.. And while this does not mean to become merely a person of rote, it does mean that each of these changes and each of these activities makes for the creating of a better balance. This not only facilitates the individual's activities, but gives the ability to concentrate, when so desiring, on whatever the activity may be."   No. 440

[16]

ENERGY BUILDING FOODS

Pure beef juice was indicated as one of the best blood building and energy producing foods. To obtain the proper results the following method of preparation must be followed carefully.

"Take a pound to a pound and a half, preferably of the round steak—no fat, no portions other than that which is of the muscle or tendon, no fatty or skin portions—dice this into half-inch cubes. Put same in a glass jar without water. Put the jar, then, into a boiler or container, with the water coming about half or three-fourths toward the top of the jar. Preferably put a cloth in the container to prevent the jar from cracking. Do not seal the jar tight but cover the top. Let this boil—the water with the jar in same—for three to four hours.

"Then strain off the juice, and the refuse may be pressed somewhat. It will be found that the meat or flesh itself will be worthless. Place the juice in a cool place, but do not keep too long; never longer than three days.

"Take a tablespoonful (sip slowly) two or three times each day. Season to suit taste.

Whole wheat or Ry-Krisp crackers may be taken with it to make it more palatable." No. 1343

SEMI-LIQUID DIET FOR STRENGTH

"....such foods as Junket, Arrowroot.... yolk of an egg well beaten with a little milk, or with milk and a little sherry or spiritus frumenti as a stimulant. Not so much of the white of the egg should be beaten in same. Take often as sips, not spoonsful. No. 2041

GELATIN

"It isn't the vitamin content (of gelatin) that is valuable but it is its ability to work with the activities of the glands, causing the glands to take from that which is absorbed or digested the vitamins that would not be active in the body if there is not sufficient gelatin in the body." No. 849

"Have a great deal of such foods as liver, tripe, pigs' knuckle, pigs' feet and the like; a great deal of okra and its products, a great deal of any form of desserts carrying quantities of gelatin. Any of the gelatin products, though they may carry sugars at times....these are to be had oft in the diet." No. 2520.

In the balanced meals given in the first section of this booklet you will find references to gelatin products. Such references occurred so often that the importance is obvious.

"In an alkalin system there is less effect of cold and congestion." No. 270

ACID AND ALKALINE FOODS

ACID FORMING

"All of those that are combining fats with sugars. Starches naturally are inclined to produce acid reaction." No. 1523

ALKALINE REACTIONS

"Lemon juice is a good alkalizer. Squeeze a little lime with it also, just two or three drops in a full glass of the lemon juice taken. Best to mix the lemon juice with water, of course. Use half a lemon or a full lemon to a glass of water, depending upon how soon the lemon is used after it is fully ripened...." No. 1709

BALANCE ACCORDING TO ACTIVITY

"For in all bodies, the less activities there are in physical exercise or manual activity, the greater should be the alkalin-reacting foods taken. Energies or activites may burn acids; but those who lead the sedentary or non-active life cannot go on sweets or too many starches. These should be carefully balanced." No. 798

[19]

EXHAUSTION

*"Do not tax the body mentally when
physically tired, and do not overtax the
body physically when mentally tired."*

No. 220

AVOID THESE COMBINATIONS

All of these suggestions were repeated many times, in different readings.

CITRUS FRUIT AND CEREALS

"....When cereals are taken, do not have citrus fruits at the same meal."　　No. 3823

COFFEE AND MILK

"Do not take milk or cream in coffee or in tea."　　No. 1568

BREAD, POTATOES, SPAGHETTI

"Do not combine white bread, potatoes, spaghetti, or any two foods of such types in the same meal."　　No. 1568

FRIED FOODS

"Do not eat fried foods of any kind." No. 1568

STARCH AND MEATS

"Do not eat great quantities of starch with proteins or meats......Small quantities of breads with sweets are all right, but do not have large quantities of them. Do not combine also the alkalin-reacting, acid fruits with starches, other than whole wheat bread."　　No. 416

"Meats should not be taken with starches that grow above the ground....Hence potatoes or potato peelings with meats are much prefer-

[21]

able to eating breads with meats.'' No. 340
''Do not use bacon or fats in cooking vegetables.'' No. 303

OTHER PUBLICATIONS

BOOKS

There Is A River, The story of Edgar
Cayce, by Thomas Sugrue, 2nd
edition, 453 pp. 3.50
What I Believe, Six Talks by Edgar
Cayce, 94 pages 1.00
A Search For God, Extracts from readings. 145 pages 1.50

PRINTED BOOKLETS

Am I My Brother's Keeper, Readings
on World Affairs. 80 pages .... .50
Meditation—First chapter in A Search
For God. 12 pages .... .25
Auras, An Essay on Color by Edgar
Cayce. 26 pages .... .25
Eat To Live, Extracts from readings
on diet. 22 pages .... .35
(3 for $1.00)

*Mimeographed list of other publications
on request.*

Order from:
The Edgar Cayce Publishing Company, Inc.,
Virginia Beach, Va.

.

CPSIA information can be obtained
at www.ICGtesting.com
Printed in the USA
BVHW04s0153011018
528924BV00019B/312/P

9 781163 171431